The Golden Goose

Retold by Brenda Parkes
Illustrated by David Pearson

Once upon a time, a mother and her three sons lived near a forest. The two older sons were woodcutters, and every day they went into the forest to cut down trees. They were strong men and very proud of themselves.

But there was also a lot of hard work to do at home: digging, planting, and taking care of the animals. They left all this work to their younger brother, Peter. They weren't very nice to Peter. They often laughed at him and said that their jobs were much more important than his.

One morning, Peter decided to start his work early.

He finished all his work just after his brothers had left for the forest. Then he said to his mother, "Today, I'm going to go cut wood, too. I'll show everyone that I can do it as well as my brothers."

He really wanted to go, so his mother agreed. "But what will you take with you to eat?" she asked. "Your brothers didn't leave us much food."

"Bread and water will be enough," said Peter, and he quickly packed a small bundle and left, waving good-bye to his mother.

Soon, all three brothers were at work in different parts of the forest. All morning, the oldest brother chopped wood, and by lunchtime, he was ready to eat and then rest.

But as he started eating his lunch, a little man appeared and said, "Please give me something to eat and drink. I'm hungry and thirsty."

The oldest brother had a huge piece of pie and a big bottle of juice, but he wouldn't share any of his lunch. "I have worked hard, and I need all this for myself," he said angrily.

Then the little man went to the second brother and asked if he would share his lunch. But the second brother wouldn't share, either. "If I give any to you, I won't have enough for myself. Go away!" he said rudely.

When the two older brothers had finished eating, they returned to work. But, to their surprise, their axes slipped from their hands, and the heavy wooden handles fell and hit them.
They couldn't work, so they just went back home.

  Meanwhile, Peter had been working very hard, and he had chopped and stacked a huge pile of wood. His muscles hurt, but he was feeling pleased with his work.

When Peter sat down to eat, the same little man who had spoken to his brothers suddenly appeared. "Please give me something to eat and drink," he said. "I'm hungry and thirsty."

"Of course," said Peter. "But I have only a simple meal of bread and water."

Then he opened the bundle that held his lunch, and to his surprise, he saw that his simple meal had become a wonderful lunch!

After they had eaten, the little man said, "That was a fine meal you shared with me, my friend." And he told Peter that he would receive a gift for his kindness. "If you follow the path that leads to your home, you will come to an old tree that is bent and twisted. If you cut it open, you will find something very valuable."

Peter started walking along the path, and soon he came to the tree that the old man had described. He swung his axe and hit the twisted trunk. The tree opened up easily, and inside Peter saw a goose with shining feathers of pure gold! He picked it up and put it under his arm. Then he hurried home. He was excited, and he wanted to show his family what he had found.

But when he ran into the house with the golden goose, his brothers wouldn't listen to him or look at the goose. They were angry that Peter had had such good luck. The two of them had brought home nothing.

Later that night, they went into Peter's bedroom. They were very quiet. They were going to take the goose for themselves.

"We'll sell this goose," whispered one brother.
"And if we get a lot of money, we'll never have to work again," said the other. He bent down to take the goose from its basket. But as soon as he touched it, he found that his hand was stuck to the golden feathers.

"What are you doing?" whispered his brother angrily. He reached out to pick up the goose himself, but when he tried to push his brother away, he found that he was stuck to him!

The brothers pushed and pulled and turned and twisted, but they could find no way to get free.

They called their mother for help, and soon she was stuck to them, too. Then Peter was awakened by all the noise, and he found the three of them stuck together, with the goose looking very upset.

"Please do something, Peter!" cried his mother. "We're all stuck together and can't get free!"

13

Peter tried, but there was nothing he could do. So they stayed like that for hours, waiting for the sun to rise. Then they went to find someone who could help them.

They all went out of the house, still stuck together, with Peter and his goose leading the way.

They went past the forest, into the town, and down the street by the bakery. "Help me! I'm stuck!" the mother shouted to the baker, so he grabbed her, and then he was stuck, too.

They continued through the town until they passed the butcher shop, where the butcher was making sausages.

"Help me! I'm stuck!" shouted the baker, so the butcher grabbed him, and then he was stuck, too.

They went on and on, and anyone who touched them got stuck, too. They kept running on through the town until they reached the palace of the king.

The king had a daughter, who everyone called the Sad Princess. The king had promised that she would marry any man, young or old, who could make her laugh. But no one had even found a way to make her smile.

But when the princess saw Peter, with the strange bird in his arms and the silly parade of people behind him, she began to laugh and laugh. And as she laughed, all the people were freed, and there was Peter, with his golden goose, standing in front of the king.

The king was very pleased to hear his daughter laugh, but he was not pleased to see Peter. He didn't want to let his daughter marry such an ordinary young man.

So, instead of keeping his promise, the king said, "Before you may marry the princess, you must do one thing. Find me a man who can drink all the apple cider in my cellar."

Peter thought that there couldn't be any such man in the world, so he sadly started back home. But soon he met a man who said, "Please help me! I am so very thirsty. I drank up all the water in a well, but my throat is still dry!"

Peter took the man back to the palace, and soon all the king's cider was gone. But the king still wouldn't keep his promise.

Again he gave Peter an impossible job. "Now," he said, "you must find me a man who can eat a mountain of bread."

Peter felt hopeless and sadly started back home. But when he reached the forest, he met a man who said, "Please help me. I have eaten ten loaves of bread, and I am still hungry." So Peter took him back to the palace, where the man ate the mountain of bread.

Still the king would not keep his promise. "Now," he said, "I have one last job for you. You must find me a ship that can sail on land and water, and fly through the air, too. Then you may marry my daughter."

This seemed the most impossible job of all, but Peter did not feel hopeless this time. He believed that he could find what the king wanted. So Peter went back to the forest, and there he found the little man who had shown him the way to the golden goose.

"Of course I can help you," the little man told Peter. "I have already given you the ship that the king wants."

As he said this, he pointed to the golden goose. Peter watched as the bird changed into a beautiful ship with shining golden wings and sails.

Standing proudly on the ship, Peter sailed back to the palace. And this time, the king kept his promise.